This Book Is Broken

by Jonathan Maier
illustrated by Victor Rivas

© 2020 Sandviks, HOP, Inc. All Rights Reserved.

No part of this publication may be reproduced, stored in any retrieval system or transmitted, in any form or by any means, electronic, mechanical or otherwise, without prior written permission of the publisher.

Printed in China.

Oh, dear! Are you here to read this book? I'm sorry, but there has been a bit of bad luck. This book fell from a very tall shelf, and now it is broken! And it was such a good book. I had the starring role—I was the princess! And I made a very fine princess if I do say so myself!

Hey, where's my crown?

Baaa?

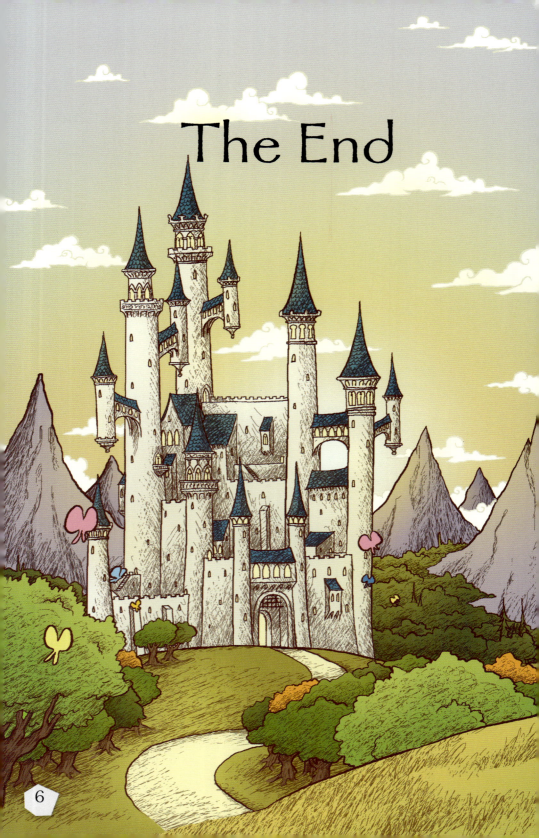

Everyone in the kingdom was very fond of the princess. No one loved her more than her dad, the king. One day he would give the princess the castle and everything that was his.

You're not the princess. You don't have a crown.

I am too the princess! I lost my crown when the book broke!

The king's brother did not like the princess. His name was Wally the Very Bad. He wanted the kingdom for his own.

Wally the Very Bad had a plan.

He said to the princess, "As you know, the king loves plums. There is a grove that no one knows about where many plums grow. They are the best plums in the kingdom."

"You must tell me how to get there," the princess said. "I will pick the plums and give them as a gift to my dad."

Ted, what are you doing here? I don't need you to save me yet. It's not time!

Wally the Very Bad gave the princess a map that pointed the way to the grove. But Wally had made up the plum story. It was really a trap to capture the princess!

The map led the princess into a deep, dark part of the kingdom. Wally's very bad men waited there for the princess.

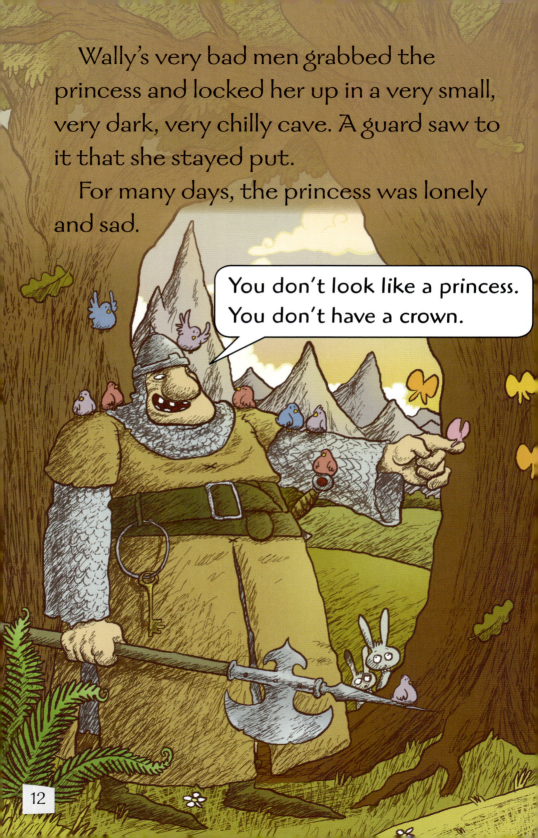

Wally's very bad men grabbed the princess and locked her up in a very small, very dark, very chilly cave. A guard saw to it that she stayed put.

For many days, the princess was lonely and sad.

You don't look like a princess. You don't have a crown.

This was Wally the Very Bad's plan. He would not let her go unless his brother, the king, gave everything he owned to Wally the Very Bad.

I'm the princess! Forget about the crown! Look at the background! It's not a cave. It's the wrong picture! It's not small or dark or chilly at all! Do I have to fix everything around here myself?

The king sent his best knight, Ted, to save the princess. Dressed as a cook, Ted put sleeping powder in the guard's dragon and spaghetti. When the guard went to sleep, Ted the Knight slipped the key from the guard's pocket and set the princess free!

"You are a princess? But you don't have—"

"A CROWN! I know, I know! Just get me out of here, would you?"

When Wally the Very Bad saw that the princess was fleeing, he shouted with anger.

"She will not get far! I will send Grogmutt the Beast to fly after her!"

The beast was very big and mean. It had a long, spiky tail and wings like black sheets. Grogmutt, you see, was a fire-breathing meatballs.

"Go, Grogmutt!" yelled Wally the Very Bad.

Meatballs?

Ted the Knight thumped Grogmutt in the noodle. The beast smacked him back with its tail. It blasted him with flames. But Ted could not be stopped. In the end, Grogmutt fled, no match for the brave knight. Ted lifted his long, gleaming sword to the sky. He had won!

That would have been a lot easier with my real sword! I lost it on that silly slide.

The princess and Ted the Knight fell in love and were married. On the wedding day, the king gave them the castle and all that he owned. Hand in hand they ruled over the land . . .

The page is upside down! That's it! I'm fed up with this. You want to keep reading the book? Fix it yourself. Sorry, but I can't take it anymore! I'm going to look for a new story where I can be a star. I will be a dentist or a soccer player—anything but a princess!

Good-bye!